Walking
With the Promises of God

RHEMA PUBLISHING
REACHING SOULS THROUGH WRITTEN TESTIMONY

Rhema Publishing Inc., Cincinnati, Ohio

Walking With the Promises of God: The Game Changer
Copyright 2015 by DeLisa Guile

All rights reserved. This book is protected by the copyright laws of the United States of America.

Scripture taken from the New Century Version®. Copyright©1987, 1988, 1991 by Thomas Nelson Inc. Used by permission. All rights reserved.

Unless otherwise indicated, Scripture quotations are from the Holy Bible, New International Version®. Copyright© 1973, 1978, 1984, 2010 by Biblica, Inc® Used by Permission of Zondervan. All rights reserved worldwide.

Scripture taken from the New King James Version. Copyright©1982 by Thomas Nelson, Inc. Used by permission. All rights reserved.

Scripture quotations marked NLT are from the Holy Bible, New Living Translation: Copyright©1996, 2004, 2007 by Tyndale House Foundation. Used by permission of Tyndale House Publishers Inc. Carol Stream, Illinois 60188. All rights reserved.

ISBN: 069242122X
ISBN-13: 978-0692421222

Walking With the Promises of God

THE GAME CHANGER

DELISA GUILE

TRUST

Proverbs 3:5-6 (NIV1984)

Trust in the Lord with all your heart and lean not on your own understanding. In all your ways acknowledge him, and he will make your paths straight.

Dear Lord,
Thank you for the Word – our ever present source of instruction, direction, encouragement and guidance.

Thank you for the timely lessons and answers to life's questions, situations, circumstances and problems.

Thanks for the consistency, the blessed assurance, the sturdy foundation. Your Word gives hope, life and knowledge. Increasing awareness, understanding of what is and expectation regarding what is to come.

Thanks for instilling peace and courage in times of change and uncertainty.

Thanks for making all things work together for my good.

GUIDANCE

Joshua 1:5 (NIV 1984)
I will never leave you nor forsake you.

Dear Lord,
Thanks for giving us your promises.

Thanks for always being true to your Word.

Thanks for always being present and aware of everything that we experience in life.

Thanks for speaking in a way your sheep can hear, and understand what we should do in every circumstance.

Thanks for always being there in ways that no one else can be or was designed to be.

LOVE

1 John 4:8 (NIV1984)
God is love.

Dear Lord,
Thanks for showing us what love is.

Thanks for showing us who love is.

Thanks for showing us in your Word what love is, how love acts and that love will last forever.

Thanks for your many ways of showing us your love.

Thanks for your ultimate sacrifice and demonstration of your unending love for us through your Son Jesus Christ.

I thank you that love, hope and faith will last forever.

And the greatest of these is love.

STRENGTH AND RENEWAL

Isaiah 40:31(KJV)
But they that wait upon the Lord shall renew their strength. They shall mount up on wings like eagles, they shall run and not grow weary, they shall walk and not faint.

Dear Lord,
Thank you for teaching us about the characteristics, mannerisms and habits of eagles.

Thank you for helping me to soar above the issues of life, renewing my hope, joy, health, dreams, and strength.

Thanks for restoration and transformation on a moment to moment basis.

Thanks for the lessons and blessings while waiting on you to do what you said you would do.

INHERITANCE

Galatians 4:7A (NLT)
And since you are his child, God has made you his heir.

Dear Lord,
Thanks for the generous daily provisions and the inheritance you bestowed and shared with me before the beginning of time.

Thank you for daily revealing to me what it means to be a child of God.

STRENGTH

Isaiah 41:10 (NIV1984)

So do not fear, for I am with you; do not be dismayed, for I am your God. I will strengthen you and help you; I will uphold you with my righteous right hand.

Dear Lord,
Thank you for giving me courage to face life's challenges and pursue goals and dreams with passion and determination.

Thanks for times of inspiration, direction and instruction.

Thanks for giving me the spirit of power, of love, and a sound mind.

CHOICES

Ephesians 5:16 (NCV)
Use every chance you have for doing good.

Dear Lord,
Thanks for the many opportunities and ways you have shown me to share whatever I have with others.

Thanks for the clear examples since my childhood.

Thanks for the many ways to show love to our neighbors.

Thanks for giving me a heart of compassion and service.

PRAISE

Psalm 34:1,8

Verse 1 (KJV)
I will bless the Lord at all times: his praise shall continually be in my mouth.

Verse 8 (KJV)
O taste and see that the Lord is good, blessed is the man who takes refuge in him.

Dear Lord,
Thanks for giving me songs in my heart and a garment of praise.

Thanks for providing refuge and rest.

Thanks for your angels you have assigned just for me.

Thanks for blessing me in ways great and small, seen and unseen, revealed and yet to come to pass.

CHOICES

Galatians 6:10 (NLT)
Whenever we have the opportunity, we should do good to everyone.

Dear Lord,
Thanks for giving me the opportunity to share and show your love to others.

Thanks for the love, support, understanding and kindness you have demonstrated to me through the Word of God and the body of Christ.

Thanks for shaping me into a useful vessel for you.

STRENGTH

Psalm 31:24 (NIV)
Be strong and take heart, all you who hope in the Lord.

Dear Lord,
Thank you for showing me what true strength is, how it is developed and displayed to the world.

Thanks for showing me in your Word how to think, live, work and interact with others.

Thanks for showing me I am chosen, I have purpose and destiny, and have victory in every situation.

PEACE

Romans 14:19 (NIV)
Make every effort to do what leads to peace and to mutual edification.

Dear Lord,
Thanks for the principles, instructions, and illustrations in your Word of how we can experience peace.

Thanks for giving me peace.

Thanks for restoring my peace.

Thanks for giving me the opportunity to be a change agent for you by speaking, writing and bringing forth peace in times of chaos, crisis, confusion and contention.

Thanks for shaping me to be an instrument of peace.

PRAISE

Psalm 34:3 (NIV)
Glorify the Lord with me: let us exalt his name together.

Dear Lord,
I thank you and bless your name for all that you are, all you have done and all you are going to do.

Thanks for being uniquely you.

I am grateful that no one else compares to you.

I will continue to give you my all, my best and use my gifts and talents to help others learn, develop and walk in relationship with you.

FORGIVENESS

Colossians 3:13 (NLT)
Make allowance for each other's faults, and forgive anyone who offends you. Remember, the Lord forgave you, so you must forgive others.

Dear Lord,
Thanks for the power of forgiveness.

Thanks for the blessings of obedience, grace and mercy.

Thanks for redeeming us through Jesus Christ.

Thanks for telling us we are forgiven, and the past is to be and has been forgotten. Thanks for the sea of forgetfulness.

Thanks for lifting, and removing stumbling stones, burdens and the spirit of heaviness.

Thanks for your lessons in your Word.

Thanks for our friendship.

TRUST

Psalm 37:4-5 (NIV)

Delight yourself in the Lord and he will give you the desires of your heart.

Commit your way to the Lord; trust in him and he will do this.

Dear Lord,
Thanks for fulfilling the spoken and unspoken desires of my heart.

Thanks that your Word does not return void.

Thanks for keeping your promises.

ASSIGNMENTS

Matthew 28:18-20 (NIV)

Jesus said, all authority in heaven and on earth has been given to me. Therefore go and make disciples of all nations, baptizing them in the name of the Father and of the Son and of the Holy Spirit, and teaching them to obey everything I have commanded you. And surely I am with you always, to the very end of the age.

Dear Lord,
Thanks for giving us instructions for life.

Thanks for your willingness and commitment to be here with us throughout our lives.

Thanks for how you teach us from day to day all that we need to know and understand.

Thanks for providing the ways to share what we have learned with others.

PRAISE

Philippians 4:8 (NIV1984)
Finally brothers, whatever is true, whatever is noble, whatever is right, whatever is pure, whatever is lovely, whatever is admirable—if anything is excellent or praiseworthy—think about such things.

Dear Lord,
Thanks for telling us clearly in the Word of God what we should think on, how we should think, what we should focus and meditate on, and how to apply it to our lives.

Our thoughts help shape our lives and behavior.

It impacts our perspectives and influences our behavior and interactions with others.

Thanks for guidance, instruction and direction.

Thanks for the transforming power of the Word of God.

PRAISE

Matthew 5:9 (NLT)
Jesus said, God blesses those who work for peace for they will be called the children of God.

Dear Lord,
Thanks for allowing me to learn, walk and work with you.

Thanks for motivating me and shaping me to be an instrument of peace instead of a carrier of strife.

PRAISE

Psalm 139:14 (NIV)

I praise you because I am fearfully and wonderfully made; your works are wonderful, I know that full well.

Dear Lord,
I praise you for your works, the ultimate creator and designer.

I thank you for being all-knowing and all-powerful.

I thank you that mankind has limitations.

I thank you that there is no one like me, for I am your unique creation, one of a kind, designed for your glory.

I am grateful that no one can compare and surpass you.

I am grateful for who you are to me, and that you are I AM to all.

LOVE

Philippians 2:3-4 (NIV1984)
Do nothing out of selfish ambition or vain conceit, but in humility consider others better than yourselves. Each of you should look not only to your own interests, but also to the interests of others.

Dear Lord,
Thank you for telling us the first and greatest commandment: to love you with all our heart, mind and soul.

Thanks for continually shaping our hearts and minds to be more like you.

Thank you for telling us to love our neighbor as ourselves.

Thanks for showing us what that means.

Thanks for not designing us to be self-centered or selfish.

FAITH

Mark 11:24 (NIV)
Therefore I tell you, whatever you ask for in prayer, believe that you have received it, and it will be yours.

Dear Lord,
Thanks for giving me hope in times of uncertainty and adversity.

Thanks for the blessed assurance.

Thanks for an ever-evolving and strengthening faith.

PEACE

Romans 12:18 (GNT)
Do everything possible on your part to live in peace with everybody.

Dear Lord,
Thanks for showing me continually how I can live in peace at all times.

Thanks for giving me peace that surpasses all understanding.

POWER OF PRAYER

John 14:14 (NIV)
You may ask me for anything in my name, and I will do it.

Dear Lord,
Thanks for your openness, willingness and generosity to listen, acknowledge and respond to everything I ask.

Thanks for the freedom of expression without any limitations.

FOCUS

Proverbs 4:23 (GNT)
Be careful how you think; your life is shaped by your thoughts.

Dear Lord,
Thanks for times and words of caution.

Thanks for prayer, wisdom and discernment.

Thanks for allowing us to change from moment to moment, becoming more of who we are destined and purposed to be.

Thanks for your faithfulness and new mercies every day.

STRENGTH

Philippians 4:13 (NKJV)
I can do all things through Christ who gives me strength.

Dear Lord,
Thanks for your words of confidence, courage and assurance.

I thank you that we don't have to live according to the viewpoints of others who have limited expectations for our lives.

I am thankful that eyes have not seen, and ears have not heard all that you have for me and what you will do.

STRENGTH

Matthew 4:4 (NIV1984)

Jesus answered, It is written: man does not live on bread alone, but on every word that comes from the mouth of God.

Dear Lord,
Thanks for providing for our growth, development and nourishment in your Word.

STRENGTH

Psalm 46:1 (NIV)
God is our refuge and strength, an ever-present help in trouble.

Dear Lord,
Thank for being my covering, helper and keeper.

Thanks for letting me know I can turn to you for everything.

PERFECTION

Proverbs 30:5 (NIV)
Every word of God is flawless.

Dear Lord,
I thank you that your Word is perfect.

I thank you because your Word is all encompassing and complete.

I thank you that your Word helps us deal with everything that happens in life.

I thank you that no one and nothing can match your Word.

I thank you that your Word is alive and has power.

ENCOURAGEMENT

Psalm 27:14 (NIV)
Wait for the Lord; be strong and take heart and wait for the Lord.

Dear Lord,
Thanks for the lessons and blessings of waiting on you.

Thanks for renewed strength and a heart of God.

FAITH IN ACTION

James 1:22 (NKJV)
But, be doers of the word, and not hearers only, deceiving yourselves.

Dear Lord,
Thanks for life applications and illustrations of the Word of God.

Thanks for showing us how we can activate the lessons and principles we learn on a daily basis.

JOY

Psalm 118:24 (NIV)

This is the day the Lord has made; let us rejoice and be glad in it.

Dear Lord,
Thank you for each and every day.

I thank you that every day is a blessing and has hope and promise.

I thank you, that just as the sky is different every day, our lives can be different as well.

Thanks for telling me and showing me the joy of the Lord is my strength.

Thanks for giving me joy and gladness.

JOY

Romans 5:3-4 (NCV)

We also have joy with our troubles, because we know that these troubles produce patience. And patience produces character, and character produces hope.

Dear Lord,

Thanks for the lessons in patience.

Thanks for reshaping my character.

Thanks for providing us a living example in Jesus of how to behave and interact with others.

JOY

Galatians 5:22-23 (NIV)
But the fruit of the Spirit is love, joy, peace, patience, kindness, goodness, faithfulness, gentleness and self-control. Against such things there is no law.

Dear Lord,
Thanks for instilling in me the gifts of the Spirit.

Thanks for allowing me to share these gifts with others.

Thanks for the reminders that we are known by the fruit we bear and show to others.

CHOICES

Romans 12:21 (NIV)
Do not be overcome by evil, but overcome evil with good.

Dear Lord,
Thanks for making me an overcomer.

Thanks for the armor of God.

Thanks for teaching me how to fight the fight of faith.

Thanks for allowing the opportunity to choose what to do and how to do it.

Thanks for being our example.

Thanks for providing the numerous parables and illustrations in the Word of God of how our walk can be and should be.

PRAISE

Psalm 118:1 (NIV)
Give thanks to the Lord, for he is good; his love endures forever.

Dear Lord,
I am forever grateful for all that you have done and are doing for me.

I am grateful that your purposes and plans prevail.

GOD'S PLANS

Ecclesiastes 3:1 (CEV)
Everything on earth has its own time and its own season.

Dear Lord,
I thank you for creating and holding time in your hands.

Thanks for the lessons along the journey.

Thanks for growth and development, changes and being molded on the potter's wheel.

I thank you that all things do not remain the same, and that Jesus Christ is the same yesterday, today and forever.

FOCUS

Psalm 19:14 (NIV)

May the words of my mouth and the meditation of my heart be pleasing in your sight, O Lord, my Rock and my Redeemer.

Dear Lord,
Life and death is in the power of spoken words.

Let me be a vessel of hope and encouragement.

Sharing words of truth with love, compassion, empathy and understanding.

FINISH

Philippians 1:6 (NIV 1984)

Being confident of this, that he who began a good work in you will carry it on to completion until the day of Christ Jesus.

Dear Lord,
Thanks for finishing what you start.

Thanks for the examples in commitment, dedication, focus, determination and perseverance.

Thanks for the assignments and being the author of my faith.

VICTORY

Romans 8:31 (NIV)

What, then, shall we say in response to this? If God is for us, who can be against us?

Dear Lord,
Thanks for your hedge of protection.

Thanks for showing me how to use the shield of faith, the helmet of salvation, the breastplate of righteousness, the belt of truth and the shoes of peace.

CHOSEN

Jeremiah 1:5 (NCV)
Before I made you in your mother's womb, I chose you. Before you were born, I set you apart for a special work.

Dear Lord,
Thanks for letting me know that I am chosen.

Thanks for the purposes and plans you designed just for me.

Thanks for letting me know when I am apart from others, I am never apart from you.

PURPOSE

Romans 8:28 (NIV)
And we know that in all things God works for the good of those who love him, who have been called according to his purpose.

Dear Lord,
Thanks for being the original planner and designer.

The ultimate architect for the world and mankind.

Your creations are masterpieces.

None can be duplicated.

Many are continually discovered.

Your works are wonderful, I know that full well.

CHOSEN

1 Peter 2:9 (GW)
However, you are a chosen people, a royal priesthood, a holy nation, people who belong to God. You were chosen to tell about the excellent qualities of God, who called you out of darkness into his marvelous light.

Dear Lord,
How excellent is your name in all the earth.

Thanks for the gifts, talents and responsibilities given specifically to me for building your kingdom.

To God be the glory for all the things He has done.

POWER OF PRAYER

John 15:7 (NIV1984)
If you remain in me and my words remain in you, ask whatever you wish, and it will be given you.

Dear Lord,
Thank you for listening to my every thought and prayer.

Thanks for the openness and being available at all times.

Thanks for your love and protection, teaching and training for life and ministry.

Thanks for being a safe place, a refuge, a safe haven and source of strength for me at all times.

POWERFUL FAITH

Matthew 21:22 (NIV)
If you believe, you will receive whatever you ask for in prayer.

Dear Lord,
I thank you that my faith has grown. Thanks for keeping me together through the difficult times and places of oppression, strife and adversity.

Thank you for giving me the opportunity to choose what to believe.

Thanks for being reliable and consistent.

I thank you that your Word does not return void.

Thanks for renewing my joy, health and strength.

Thanks for always looking out for my best and wellbeing.

GIFTS

Ephesians 4:7 (CEV)
Christ has generously divided out his gifts to us.

Dear Lord,
Thanks for your generosity. I am truly humbled and grateful that you would bestow gifts to me.

Please be patient as I grow in knowledge, responsibility and courage to gain awareness and obedience to use the gifts in the manner you intended.

FAITH

Hebrews 11:1 (NIV1984)
Now faith is being sure of what we hope for and certain of what we do not see.

Dear Lord,
Thanks for blessed assurance that You are the great I AM and you cannot lie.

Thanks for developing my confidence that I can always turn to you regarding everything. I don't have to try to learn and figure everything out on my own. I don't have to rely on the opinions of others.

Thanks for speaking to me in the many ways that you do.

Thanks for providing patience and contentment while waiting on the manifestation of your promises.

MATTERS OF THE HEART

Proverbs 27:19 (NLT)
As a face is reflected in water, so the heart reflects the person.

Dear Lord,
Thanks for revealing insight regarding other people.

I thank you the Word of God is a mirror, showing us who we are, how we are, and how we can be.

I thank you for working on my heart, giving me heart more like the heart of God.

PROVISION

Philippians 4:19 (NIV1984)
And my God will meet all your needs according to his glorious riches in Christ Jesus.

Dear Lord,
You have my love and gratitude.

I thank you for being my provider, my supplier, my resource and sustainer. Thanks for preparing my pathways.

I thank you for being all-knowing.

You know what I need before I may realize or acknowledge it.

Thanks for your grace and mercy for times and actions of futility, disobedience and impatience.

SERVICE

1 Samuel 12:20 (NCV)
Serve the Lord with all your heart.

Dear Lord,
I open and make my heart available to you.

I will serve you wholeheartedly forever.

COURAGE

Joshua 1:9 (NIV1984)
Have I not commanded you? Be strong and courageous. Do not be terrified; do not be discouraged, for the Lord your God will be with you wherever you go.

Dear Lord,
Being strong and courageous are words of action and commitment.

Thanks for teaching me what those words mean.

I thank you that I don't have to make individuals in the marketplace and the world, as my example.

GIFTS

Romans 12:6-8 (NLT)

In his grace, God has given us different gifts for doing certain things well. So if God has given you the ability to prophesy, speak out with as much faith as God has given you. If your gift is serving others, serve them well. If you are a teacher, teach well. If your gift is to encourage others, be encouraging. If it is giving, give generously. If God has given you leadership ability, take the responsibility seriously. And if you have a gift for showing kindness to others, do it gladly. The Lord gives strength to his people, the Lord blesses his people with peace.

Dear Lord,
I thank you that my gifts and abilities have come from you.

I thank you that no one can take them away from me.

Thanks for the revelation process, showing me what I can process and handle at a time.

Thanks for being patient with me during my Christian walk.

BLESSINGS

Psalm 29:11 (NIV)
The Lord gives strength to his people, the Lord blesses his people with peace.

Dear Lord,
Thanks for loving me and teaching me by example in your Word of what strength is.

Thanks for peace beyond any measure and understanding.

Thanks for letting me know what is possible, and that there are no limits in you.

Thanks for always being available.

Thanks for complete confidence and being a promise keeper.

Thanks for demonstrating your love and the plans for our lives continually in many ways of expression and illustration.

Thanks for being the ultimate teacher for all times.

I am thankful I am in your classroom on a 24 hour and 7 days a week basis.

WEALTH

Deuteronomy 8:18 (NIV1984)
Remember the Lord your God, for it is he who gives you the ability to produce wealth.

Dear Lord,
I thank you for revealing to me the TRUTH in your Word.

Since I know the truth, I am now set free. I can worship and walk in fellowship with you in spirit and in truth.

Thanks for dreams, visions, plans, assignments, discernment, gifts, talents, guidance, instruction and correction.

Thanks for letting me know that if I seek your kingdom first and all of your righteousness, you have promised to take care of me. This is a guarantee, since you do not lie, and your Word does not return empty or void. I don't have to worry about what to eat, or wear or drink. You have made provisions for the entire world and everything you have created in it for your glory. I treasure our relationship and will walk with you forever. Thanks for being patient and understanding, showing great compassion, gentleness and mercy.

PEACE

Philippians 4:6-7 (NIV1984)
Do not be anxious about anything, but in everything, by prayer and petition, with thanksgiving, present your requests to God. And the peace of God, which transcends all understanding, will guard your hearts and your minds in Christ Jesus.

Dear Lord,
I bless you and thank you for all that you are to me.

I am truly yours and amazed by just how much you love me and want the best for me.

As I reflect upon what your Word says and what I have been taught by you about you since before I was born, to this day, the love you have consistently shown gives me blessed assurance that you are mine, and I have always been in your heart, on your mind, and in your hands.

EQUIPPING

Hebrews 13:21 (NLT)

May he equip you with all you need for doing his will. May he produce in you, through the power of Jesus Christ, every good thing that is pleasing to him. All glory to him forever and ever! Amen.

Dear Lord,
Thank you for equipping me with all that I need.
I don't need to rely on other people or resources.
You give freely and completely and generously.
When I feel or think I am in lack, you quickly show all provisions and blessings are there just for the asking. Thanks for the promises and blessings bestowed upon me.

Thanks for telling me and showing me, and teaching me that I am the head and not the tail.
Thanks for telling me I will be blessed in the city and blessed in the field, blessed wherever I go.
I thank you that your Word does not return void and that you are not selective in the blessings.
Thank you for your commands and your hedge of protection.
Thanks for providing the standards.

STRENGTH

Psalm 18:32 (NIV1984)
It is God who arms me with strength and makes my way perfect.

Dear Lord,
Thank you for providing guidance, insight and direction.

Thanks for building my strength and character.

Thanks for preparing my pathways and ordering my footsteps.

Thanks for times of reflection, assessment and redirection.

Thanks for revelation of truth and opportunities ahead.

Thanks for being the author and finisher of my faith.

GOD'S PLANS

2 Corinthians 1:4 (NCV)
He comforts us in all our troubles so that we can comfort others. When others are troubled, we will be able to give them the same comfort God has given us.

Dear Lord,
Thanks for providing comfort in times of loss, frustration and disappointment.

Thanks for giving me compassion and patience to listen and be supportive to others. May others be drawn to you as a result.

Thanks for increasing empathy and understanding.

Thanks for giving me insight and wisdom.

GOD'S PLANS

Jeremiah 29:11-13 (NIV1984)
For I know the plans I have for you, declares the Lord, plans to prosper you and not to harm you, plans to give you hope and a future. Then you will call upon me and come and pray to me, and I will listen to you. You will seek me and find me when you seek me with all your heart.

Dear Lord,
Thanks for your openness and willingness to always be available to listen.

Thanks for addressing each and every prayer I lift to you.

Thanks for your plans prepared just for me. Thanks for sharing the details in an interesting and unfolding manner.

Thanks for the assignments and increasing ability and confidence to fulfill the destiny available to me.

Thanks for reassurance that prosperity will be a part of my testimony and an extension of my contribution to the world.

PERSERVERANCE

Hebrews 12:1 (NIV1984)

Therefore, since we are surrounded by such a great cloud of witnesses, let us throw off everything that hinders and the sin that so easily entangles, and let us run with perseverance the race marked out for us.

Dear Lord,
Thanks for showing me the freedom and joy that comes from laying aside the extra weights.

Thanks for equipping me and being my coach as I pace myself, focused ahead with excitement and determination to move forward with a guaranteed victory.

May I be mindful and diligent, releasing and sidestepping any hindrances which may impact and alter how I run the race.

JOY

1 Thessalonians 5:16-18 (NIV)
Be joyful always; pray continually; give thanks in all circumstances for this is God's will for you in Christ Jesus.

Dear Lord,
Thanks you for giving me joy, even during challenging and difficult circumstances. I realize it is possible, important and essential to maintain the presence of joy. It is gift embedded deep within my heart. It springs up and changes the atmosphere and my perspective in ways I cannot fully comprehend, but graciously appreciate.

Thanks for the ability and opportunity to pray about everything and everyone—placing our futures in your hands. You answer, fix, and take care of all our wants and needs.

Thanks for your generosity.

LOVE

Philippians 1:9 (NLT)
I pray that your love will overflow more and more, and that you will keep on growing in knowledge and understanding.

Dear Lord,
Thanks for increasing my patience, compassion and understanding. The growth process has been life-changing. The lessons have been continual. The level of knowledge and insight is always amazing and surprising.

May I continue to be persistent, committed and focused with the plans your have prepared for me.

May I continue to learn what love looks like from your perspective, and actively demonstrate and share it with others, everywhere I go.

GUIDANCE

Psalm 119:105 (NIV1984)
Your word is a lamp to my feet and a light for my path.

Dear Lord,
Thank you for the Word. It provides guidance, instruction and clarity regarding how to approach and interpret the choices and experiences in life.

The life plan has been a game changer.

FRUIT

Matthew 7:16 (CEV)
You can tell what they are by what they do.

Dear Lord,
Thanks for providing awareness and a greater understanding of the individuals and environments I have been associated with.

At times, the situations and circumstances seemed very surprising, overwhelming, distinct and unfamiliar. The learning experiences have been challenging and purposeful.

Being an observer and listening more than speaking has proved beneficial.

I understand and appreciate more and more why we are instructed to be quick to listen and slow to speak.

Our behavior and content of our conversation tells a compelling story.

FAITH

Romans 10:17 (NIV1984)
Consequently, faith comes from hearing the message, and the message is heard through the word of Christ.

Dear Lord,
Thanks for the many lessons and chances to hear from you.

Thanks for the growth in the walk and fight of faith.

Thanks for providing points of comparison of what you have said in your Word, versus the words spoken by people.

Thanks for clarity and discernment. Thanks for the ability to hear, listen, process, retain and filter information.

Thanks for the ability to decipher the truth against the opinions, attitudes and perspectives of various speakers. The desire to have an audience, persuade and influence others can reveal agendas apart from God's intended purpose and plans. Help your children to be better vessels and ambassadors for you — serving in a manner pleasing in your sight.

TAKING ACTION

Proverbs 3:28 (GNT)
Never tell your neighbors to wait until tomorrow if you can help them now.

Dear Lord,
Thanks for giving us the motivation, willingness and ability to reach, respond and share with others. Delays and procrastination impacts others in a measure we cannot ignore or overlook.

Since you are not hesitant to show comfort, care, concern and provision to us, we should in turn remember your gracious and loving acts, and be inspired to improve the lives and wellbeing of other people. We are clearly instructed to love our neighbors as ourselves. Let us be continually stretched to a greater capacity to show love in action. The world will see you by the love we extend to all.

PEACE

John 14:27 (NIV1984)

Peace I leave with you; my peace I give to you. I do not give to you as the world gives. Do not let your hearts be troubled and do not be afraid.

Dear Lord,
Thanks for giving us peace. It is something we need at all times.

Peace is a precious and treasured gift that you have freely and abundantly chosen to give to us.

It settles within us and overcomes the chaos around us. It has the power to transform hearts, mindsets and atmospheres like nothing else. Your peace encompasses anything we could ask for.

Thank you for allowing peace to rest upon us and radiate within us. I thank you that the peace you give is evident to all.

I am glad and grateful that no one and nothing can change what you have given to us. Let us be humble and strive to walk in peace with other people and especially within ourselves.

TRUST

Luke 16:10 (NIV1984)
Whoever can be trusted with very little can also be trusted with much, and whoever is dishonest with very little will also be dishonest with much.

Dear Lord,

Thank you for the lessons in faithfulness and measures of trustworthiness. This has served as a guide in making decisions in personal and professional life. It has also served as an instrument for assessing character, ethics, priorities and ambitions.

The instructions, pressures and opportunities to make wrong and unfavorable decisions have led many along paths they could not imagine or escape from. The pain, trauma and consequences have been considerable.

The chance for redemption and restoration has been a gift and blessing for all individuals-- too numerous to count.

Celebrating the return and recovery of what was lost or missing is a joyous occasion for each one of us to partake and experience.

BLESSINGS

Ephesians 1:3 (NIV1984)
Praise be to the God and Father of our Lord Jesus Christ, who has blessed us in the heavenly realms with every spiritual blessing in Christ.

Dear Lord,
Thank you for your provisions and preparations made for us, your children. I thank you that we are heirs by your unalterable choice and declaration.

Thank you for your unending blessings. Thank you for seeing us for who you purposed and destined for us to be, from our very beginning.

Thank you for revealing to me the various ways you have strategically placed and designed your blessings intended particularly for me. I am awestruck, excited and deeply moved by your extended and outreached hands toward me.

I will continually give you honor and praise.

JOY

Psalm 100:2 (NIV1984)
Worship the Lord with gladness; come before him with joyful songs.

Dear Lord,
Thank you for giving me the opportunity to come before you with honor, humility, joy and praise.

Thanks for giving me songs in my heart. I thank you that my joy is always present, regardless of external circumstances. I thank you for the gladness that I cannot limit, contain or withhold. I share it openly for all the world to see.

It is important to always remember that I have an audience of one — my only focus and source of strength.

JOY

Proverbs 17:22A (NIV 1984)
A cheerful heart is good medicine.

Dear Lord,
Thank you for the transforming power of joy and laughter. A physician shared this scripture with me a very long time ago.

Over time I experienced and understood the truth from these gifts giving priceless and intangible shifts in perspective, thoughts, emotions and environments from the smiles and cheerfulness flowing from myself and others.

The amazing reality is that we cannot always reach out to others for a boost or encouragement.

I am so glad I can reflect on wonderful memories and encourage myself when necessary.

GOD'S POWER

Isaiah 55:9 (NIV1984)
As the heavens are higher than the earth, so are my ways higher than your ways and my thoughts than your thoughts.

Dear Lord,
Thank you for being above the abilities and ambitions of mankind. Considerable time and resources have been devoted and expended that were not within your purpose and plans. Just like the individuals in the Bible who decided to build towers and erect statutes and other structures by the works of their hands, we too have limitations.

Thank you for your wisdom. Our behavior and choices surely don't take you by surprise. I pray we become more intrigued and respectful regarding who you are. We are vessels to be shaped by eternal design, never to be duplicated or flawed.

We are your spoken word, therefore we should see ourselves as whole and flawless.

GIFTS FROM GOD

2 Timothy 1:7 (NKJV)
For God did not give us a spirit of fear, but a spirit of power, of love and a sound mind.

Dear Lord,
Thank you for removing fear and instilling courage, stability, confidence and a loving heart. Thank you for removing conflict, regret, bitterness and doubt.

Thank you for working all things together for my good. Thank you for all the written examples and history of giving continually and generously to us—your children. Thank you that every good and perfect gift comes from above.

I thank you that we do not have to remain stuck in challenging situations. Thanks for the power and ability to keep moving forward.

STRENGTH

2 Corinthians 12:10 (NCV)
For this reason I am happy when I have weaknesses, with insults, and distresses, with persecutions, with difficulties for Christ's sake; for when I am weak , then I am strong.

Dear Lord,
Thanks for the opportunity to learn and grow from experiences. As someone who has a passion for learning, I may not always appreciate the processes and problems presented to me at the time.

Reflections, guidance, insight and prayers have made a significant impact. We only gain strength when we are stretched and challenged. Strength is built by repetitions and resistance.

Let us persevere and yield to the training exercises you allow us to go through. We know we will be victorious in the end.

STRENGTH

Psalm 55:22 (NIV1984)
Cast your cares on the Lord and he will sustain you; he will never let the righteous fall.

Dear Lord,
Thank you for allowing us the privilege and freedom to be able to share cares, concerns and burdens with you.

Thanks for being available, willing and able to handle and respond to everything we present before you. Thank you for removing weights that we were never intended to carry.

Thanks for times and areas of renewal and strengthening. Thanks for increased endurance, determination, commitment and resilience.

Thanks for the outpouring of your love, guidance and protection.

STRENGTH

Isaiah 40:29 (NIV1984)
He gives strength to the weary and increases the power of the weak.

Dear Lord,
Thank you for times of rest, renewal, reflection and strengthening. Taking time to rest establishes balance, peace, creativity, and a better perspective on the circumstances and opportunities present before me.

Thanks for direction and strategies to successfully overcome challenges. It is clearly shown in your Word, the patterns and track record of success.

I believe I can continue to be an achiever and accomplish the plans, goals and visions within me.

WAITING ON GOD

Romans 8:25-26 (NIV1984)
But if we hope for what we do not yet have, we wait for it patiently. In the same way, the Spirit helps us in our weakness. We do not know what we ought to pray for, but the Spirit himself intercedes for us with groans that words cannot express.

Dear Lord,
Thanks for intercession on my behalf. I am grateful that you know and fully understand what I need.

Thanks for giving me patience. It is serving me well. It may not always feel comfortable, but I realize there are benefits and blessings associated with patience. Delays are not necessarily bad experiences, and can lead to the best experiences.

Thank you for your favor.

TRUST

Psalm 9:10 (NIV1984)
Those who know your name will trust in you, for you, Lord, have never forsaken those who seek you.

Dear Lord,
Thank you for showing me I can continually trust you. Since you are consistent and stable, I can always rely on you. Since you are the same today, yesterday and forever, I am always a priority to you. You are always available to listen and respond to my prayers.

May others discover these truths in their walk.

TRUST

John 15:9-12 (NIV1984)

As the Father has loved me, so have I loved you. Now remain in my love. If you obey my commands, you will remain in my love, just as I have obeyed my Father's commands and remain in his love. I have told you this so that my joy may be in you and that your joy may be complete. My command is this: Love each other as I have loved you.

Dear Lord,
Thank you for giving me reminders and instructions of where my focus should be. Your commands are given for many reasons— the primary motivation is based on your love for us.

Thank you for giving me complete joy. It is always accessible and present. I need to always remember this truth and celebrate the precious gift you have given to me.

JOY

Psalm 33:21 (NIV1984)
In him our hearts rejoice, for we trust in his holy name.

Dear Lord,
Thanks for showing me that I can trust in you and the power of the name of Jesus.

Thank you for listening, responding, and taking action when I look to you. Thank you for strengthening my faith. Thank you for helping me in ways that others cannot fully grasp or understand.

Thank you for our unique relationship. Thanks you for all that you are to me. Thank you for all that you have done for me. Thank you for all you are doing through me.

Thank you for the plans and provisions you have made for me.

PURPOSE

John 21:25 (NLT)

There are many other things Jesus did also. If they were all written down, I do not think the world itself could hold all the books that would be written.

Dear Lord,
Thanks for revealing to me in a special way the gifts, talents, assignments, and lasting impressions you designed just for me.

Thanks for making the outflow and expression from my heart a catalyst and resource to help uplift and encourage others in their daily walk. It is amazing to reflect and remember various aspects of this journey. I never could have imagined how everything could come together and have purpose and meaning to improve my life and bless others in the process.

You are awesome and I am grateful for all that you are and all that you are doing in my life.

BLESSINGS

Proverbs 9:11 (NIV1984)
For through me your days will be many, and years will be added to your life.

Dear Lord,
Thank you for making life new, interesting, exciting and increasingly better. Each day is a special occasion.

We need to select a positive perspective. Each day has promises, blessings, opportunities and expectations to be met or surpassed.

Thank you for making all things excellent. Everything you have created is a masterpiece—including us, your children.

May we see our significance and greatness through your Word and commit to sharing our praise and appreciation, as we move forward in authority, power and victory.

CHOSEN

1 Peter 2:9 (NIV1984)

But you are a chosen people, a royal priesthood, a holy nation, God's special possession, that you may declare the praises of him who called you out of darkness into his wonderful light.

Dear Lord,
Thank you for showing me I have been chosen. I share my praises to you to let all know you have wonderful and amazing plans for the them. Your generosity and graciousness, we cannot fully comprehend. We are always in your care, even when we do not realize or recognize this fact, at the time.

Thanks for loving us beyond measure. Thanks for your patience. Thanks for giving us guidance and wisdom.

Thanks for changing and reshaping us from moment to moment for your glory and your vision for our lives.

PURPOSE

2 Corinthians 3:2-3 (NIV1984)
You yourselves are our letter, written on our hearts, known and read by everybody. You show that you are a letter from Christ, the result of our ministry, written not with ink but with the Spirit of the living God, not on tablets of stone but on tablets of human hearts.

Dear Lord,
Thank you for our connection—your relationship with me and the one reading these words.

Thank you for the work and the walk you have given us. May we continue to show your love to others in new and increasing measures.

May it be so evident that no one will question your power and presence in our lives.

Thank you for loving us beyond our understanding. We take joy and comfort in it.

May we follow your example of accepting people where they are, and showing love without limitations.

May we be more effective in connecting others with you so they may experience your unending love.

PURPOSE

Acts 1:8 (NLT)
But you will receive power when the Holy Spirit comes upon you. And you will be my witnesses, telling people about me everywhere—in Jerusalem, throughout Judea, in Samaria and to the ends of the earth.

Dear Lord,
Thank you for being faithful and trustworthy. Thank you for providing us with the ultimate power available to us as a gift fulfilling prophecy, promises and a far-reaching purpose.

Thanks for sharing with me the game changer. Everything has new meaning and relevance. Hidden answers are being disclosed. New ideas and strategies are being revealed. May the people of the earth hear, seek, ask and find you in their time of need.

PROTECTION

Psalm 32:7-8 (NIV1984)

You are my hiding place; you will protect me from trouble and surround me with songs of deliverance. I will instruct you and teach you in the way you should go; I will counsel you and watch over you.

Dear Lord,

Thank you for shielding and covering me in the midst of trouble, danger and deep disappointment.

Thank you for giving me joy and praise through every circumstance. Thank you for giving me songs, melodies, and music to carry me through to this day.

Thank you for all that you have taught me. Thank you for the manner in which you allow me to gain patience, compassion, wisdom and understanding.

PRAYER

Jeremiah 33:2-3 (NIV1984)

This is what the Lord says, he who made the earth, the Lord who formed it and established it—the Lord is his name. Call to me and I will answer you and tell you great and unsearchable things you do not know.

Dear Lord,
Thank you for always being available to respond to my questions and prayers. I am a very inquisitive individual—always seeking knowledge, insight and understanding. This characteristic has proved beneficial and motivational in many areas of my life.

Thank you for helping to shape and re-shape my faith, attitude and perceptions. This shifting has considerably improved my outlook and outward expressions.

Thank you for inspirations, answers, ideas, strategies, plans and visions.

Thank you for being my favorite teacher.

BLESSINGS

2 Chronicles 15:7 (NIV1984)
But as for you, be strong and do not give up, for your work will be rewarded.

Dear Lord,
Thank you for the work you have given me to complete. It is challenging, interesting, fulfilling and meaningful.

It is fascinating to see how my life and the wellbeing of others can be changed, by following your guidelines and promises. It has been a treasure to learn I can trust you and your Word.

You have clearly shown yourself to be consistent, reliable and faithful. I shall continue to persevere, with expectation, assurance and confidence to see transformed and blessed individuals and environments everywhere I go.

BLESSINGS

Psalm 128:2 (NIV1984)
You will eat the fruit of your labor; blessings and prosperity will be yours.

Dear Lord,
Thank you for giving me peace, joy, strength, laughter, and the many intangible and immeasurable blessings. They are precious and priceless.

Thank you for allowing me to experience prosperity in all things. It is important for us to define, recognize and express what prosperity feels like for each individual.

Blessings and prosperity come from you. You own everything. We are blessed by your generosity. You willingly share with us—your heirs—your children.

May we follow your example and extend your love to the world.

LOVE

Matthew 22:37-39 (NIV1984)

Jesus replied, love the Lord your God with all your heart and with all your soul and with all your mind. This is the first and greatest commandment. And the second is like it, Love your neighbor as yourself.

Dear Lord,
Thank you for making our responsibilities and missions clear. The commands are essential, because we tend to be self-absorbed and self-focused.

Our relationship with you, impacts our relationship with everyone else.

May we commit to build, strengthen and improve the lives of our neighbors as we continue forward in our journey.

BLESSINGS

Proverbs 22:4 (NIV1984)

Humility and the fear of the Lord bring wealth and honor and life.

Dear Lord,
Thank you for reminding us of the importance of being humble and respectful.

Pride and arrogance lead to problems and conflicts, which could be avoided. We tend to learn our lessons easier when our mindset is in a better and reverent disposition.

Thank you for showing us the rewards and benefits of walking with your promises.

1 John 5:14-15 (NIV1984)

This is the confidence we have in approaching God; that if we ask anything according to his will, he hears us. And if we know that he hears us—whatever we ask—we know that we have what we asked of him.

Dear Lord,
Thank you for the one reading this heartfelt expression. They are truly a treasure.

Thank you for the transforming power of laughter and overflowing presence of joy. May this day and those ahead be times of abundant celebration, for every moment is a special occasion—a gift designed just for us.

May our joy increase, and may others be uplifted, inspired and changed as a result.

www.ingramcontent.com/pod-product-compliance
Lightning Source LLC
Chambersburg PA
CBHW031412040426
42444CB00005B/537